Chocolate Tears, Tears No More;

A Brother's Poetic Memoirs of His Journey To Love.

By Beloved Shamek Allah

COPYRIGHT 2007, by Beloved Shamek Allah
All rights reserved. This book may not be reproduced in any form or by any means, without written permission from the author and publisher.
ISBN 978-0-6151-8652-8

DEDICATION

I dedicated this book to my beautiful wife and our children because no matter how rough the storm was, they stuck by me when others were nowhere to be found; and also to a woman who has been a mother above all others: "Heavenly," mom you are no longer here yet you will always have a place within my heart.

Peace love is love

Beloved Sha

Taste of Heaven

Black woman if I could count each drop of rain as a moment in time, my love would be defined as having no limitations.
Black woman if I were 2 paint a picture of your beauty I would color it love.
Black woman if I had 2 describe the joy u bring me I would say it's like heaven on earth, and as sweet as honey 2 this Blackman lips.

Contents

Taste of Heaven 3

My Mother My Shorty & Best Friend 6

Part I (Chocolate Tears) 7

Remember/Flashback of a Love Lost 8

What About Me? 9

Fu3k It 10

Trick/ The Devils Talking P1 11

Suicidal Thoughts P1 12

Trick/Devil Still Talking P2 13

Better Days 15

N!gger Please/Fatherless Child 16

Incarcerated Scar Faces 17

Vicky/Growing Up Fast 18

Truth B Told 20

Paper Chase 21

My Body 22

Conflicting Thoughts 23

Don't Tell Me 24

Sh!t Is Real 25

Burnt Out 26

Damn Damn Damn 27

Moving On/Letting Go 28

Black Girl Lost 29

Part II (Tears No More) 30

Confession 31

Insatiable 31

I Slipped 32

Not all Men 33

How Many 34

Reality 36

P.M.S.N 37

Suicidal Thoughts P2	38
Brown Eyes	39
A Good Woman	40
Drama	41
Let's Not Get It Twisted/I'm Not Them	42
The Rabbit Died	43
Can I?	44
Cross The Line P1	45
Just A Minute	46
I'm Twisted	47
Diamond In The Rough	48
Line Crossed P2	49
Tongue Tied	50
Thinking of U	51
Where I Want 2b/ Should B	52
New Birth	53
The Dawn Of Creation	54
Hot All Over 4 Fertile	55
Hell Of A Woman	56
Can't Breathe Without U	57
What?	58
If God Was A Woman	59
Chocolate Sunday	60
All That U Need	61
I Promise	62
Blessed	64
The Love of A Blackman	65
True Woman	66
My Precious Jewel	67
Thank U Baby	68
I Pray	69
No more Tears	70
Sweet Dreams	71

Dedicated to my Mother, "Heavenly"
who returned to the Essence,
but shall Never be Forgotten,
Thank you for Believing in Me.

My Mother My Shorty & Best Friend
12- 9-05

My mother was a lil woman
yet she had a lot of heart.
I call her my shorty, though she wasn't my woman she played the part.

U see she always held a brotha down since day 1;I was more than proud then 2b her son;

If she had a dollar she gave me half;
and at times I got out of line she made it born she would and could still whip my a$$.

She was there when I needed
some1 with whom I could vibe,
and she always let me know if I ever had beef she was down 4 the ride.

it was she who educated me on how 2 treat a woman like a lady
and always speak my mind.

My best friend was my mom 4 she schooled me on what a true woman was
and what, in her eyes, a true man should be,
although she's physically gone she will always be a part of me.

This Blackwoman was my mother and father, always putting me and my lil sis 1st
unlike so many lost females or weak a$$ men who said fu3k their seeds as they ran around
getting high or obeying their thirst;

She walked like a woman, spoke like a lady yet would get ghetto on that a$$
if some1 laid a hand on her precious babies--just blackout and go crazy.

I'm talking about me, "Beloved"
and my lil sista "Refined."
Mom, your not here anymore yet I think about u all the time.

Part I (Chocolate Tears)

*"Sometimes, no matter how hard you love, or how sincere you are in loving
a person, you just have to let go; because if he or she can't
respect your love, accept your love ,and return your love,
ask yourself does he or she <u>deserve</u> your love?"*

Beloved Sha

Remember/Flashback of a Love Lost

I can remember a time
when we both had nothing;
Damn, now it seems like those were the days.
I remember a time when if I had a dime
sh!t u had half.

Yes I do remember us fighting;
I also recall u getting with others,
then having the nerve 2 say u love me.
I remember us not being perfect,
but still doing whatever we had 2,
so we would have a food 2 eat.

I remember flippin' rocks
on a block that stayed hot getting chased by the cops running up in drug spots,
coming home with people's blood on my clothes…
and u not giving a damn if I stopped
or got shot.

I remember me flippin' weight and going up state I recall u not wanting 2 wait.
I remember our children's father being missing in action 4 I was doing a bid;
I remember u out in the street looking 4 some action.

I remember me putting my life on hold so u could get yours 2gether,
I can recall the police putting me on the floor and me calling u,
and u being like"n!gger whatever."

I can remember the day I wised up
and walked out the door
4 my mother was so right,
u were in love with the street
and I was 2 blind 2c u just wanted 2b a whore.

What About Me?

As a result of the pain I had endured in a meaningless relationship
I placed u upon the highest shelf, far above any1 else thus loving u more then life it self.
I surrendered my heart 2 u, and I gave my humble life 2 u never once asking what about me?
I tried 2 build a kingdom just 4 u, I tried 2b the perfect man just 4 u.
I sacrificed and compromised just 4 u, never asking once what about me?
U wrote the script, I portrayed the part, u played the music, I did the dancing,
never once asking; what about me?
U lit the fire; I'm the 1 that was burned. U made the incision, I'm the 1 that bled.
U started the war, I'm the 1 u destroyed
never once asking " what about me?"

Fu3k It

It's been almost 4 years since I've been out .
I've done all within my power 2 provide food, clothing, and shelter 4 our lil happy home.
Yet the more I try the more I feel a piece of this man dying.

1999 will either make or break me;
I want 2 get my family up out the projects,
move my fam 2 a place where they can B safe
not a place where cats get shot every other day, or people r pissing the stairway.

Yo something has 2 give, I'm about ready 2 get on some any means necessary sh!t,
but what about my kids?
The way I see it it's just me facing all of these trials and tribulations,
I need 2 put things in order and have some kind of direction.
I have 2 think about my kids…
2 old 2b doing another bid
yet I'm not 2 far from turning
n2 a stick up kid.

I'm no longer in the game I see how so much sh!t has changed,
how so-called thugs and wannabe killers have thrown salt all in the game
just 4 a lil paper and a name.
I don't want 2 live this way, being unable 2 provide 4 my kids and their mother;
yet being a Blackman with a record is just hard on a brotha .
No I don't want 2 get back in the game of being chased by the cops
getting shot or bailed out of jail,
fu3k being a thug
I'm just keeping it real.
I'm stuck between a rock and a hard place;
just trying 2 survive in this here everyday rat race.

Trick/ The Devils Talking P1

My brotha' pull up a seat
4 it's about time we meet;
I'm the other man, yes the 1 who B twisting ya baby mama back out,
and putting those marks on her neck.

2 u she's your baby mama but 2 me she just another... what's the word? Trick!
I'm the reason she gets her nails and hair done every week leaven u all alone,
yes I'm the other person on the phone, who has her closing her eyes and licking her lips,
U call her your baby mama, but 2 me she's just a trick.

My man she gives me money pays my rent, who do u think bought me this outfit?
This female doesn't give a damn about u,
open up ya eyes and stop being a fool.
B4 u think I'm stepping 2 me, your best bet is 2 step 2 her, her and I are just crushing
you're the fool in love.

Ask yourself if she's really working all those hours then where's the money?
Stop being a dummy!
Truth is she's at my house or in my car getting her back blown out.
She goes crazy 4 this d!ck;
u call her your baby mama, but 2 me she's
just another trick.

I know that at 1time u were making big bucks;
look man all she wants is 2b fu3ked.
I'm the same person she went away with 2 Atlantic City last week.
I'm the reason u and her don't speak.

I'm telling U 4 she never will,
she's not about 2 4 she wants u home takin' care of the kids.
Know this-- your baby's mama
came on 2 me.

If after what I told u,
u stay with her you're real dumb.
She calls me after she make sure u and the kids are off 2 school and work
then she get's with me so I can put in work.
If u stay with her you're a$$ is crazy—
I have 2 go now that's her paging me.

Suicidal Thoughts P1

I'm haven suicidal thoughts.
I lost my job, I have a child I can't see,
but her mother keeps telling me she needs more child support.

The female I have been with
4 most of my life
has been creeping with some cat in jail where she works-- sh!t has me smoking weed
2 ease the hurt.

Suicidal thoughts, if I could close my eyes and just rest, put an end 2 all the stress that's so heavy on my chest,
things would B so fine then I would have peace of mind.

Suicidal thoughts. Time is ticking,
but u cats aren't listening.
How could things B so right
then go so wrong?
Now I'm just another brotha'
who's singing a sad song.

Suicidal thoughts. Sh!t closing in on me, my back is against the wall;
I feel like just ending it all.

Suicidal thoughts, my bills are haven babies, sh!t 4 a brotha is just crazy.
The fall of the World Trade,
my aunt and uncle both dying from aids.

Where's the justice and where's the peace?
Amerikkka is dying slowly
as our youth run the streets.
Here I sit in a 1 bedroom with no fu3ken heat.
Ready 2 take matters n2 my own hands
2 make ends meet.

As the president just keeps starting more bullsh!t wars and the
mayor isn't doing jack,
but making bullsh!t laws.
Suicidal thoughts.

Trick/Devil Still Talking P2

So your still with her damn, how sad.
How could u stay with her knowing the next man is tapping that a$$?
The only thing I can think of it has 2b the kids, what it's been about a year?
I heard she might B haven a baby.
If you think its yours…
then I know that you're crazy!

Look she's your baby mama,
but 2 me she is just a trick,
I understand she was showing damn near all of Brooklyn some love.
If u still want 2 stay with her
then you're nuts.

I want u 2 hear me out--we started out friends, but we were never lovers.
Sh!t when I met u 2 I was still livin'
with my baby's mother.
2 u she's your baby's mama
but 2 me she is just a trick.
Girl is just a whore. I'm not the only 1st at the job-- I know of about 4!
Yo get off that "it's cheaper 2 keep her" sh!t and let that a$$ go;
2 u she's your baby mama
yet 2 everyone else she's the project hoe.
I'm just the other man
with nothing 2 hide u know?
Brotha' move on!

The Spark

The spark that once gave this heart love
is now gone; now here I contemplate
on how shall I move on.

Things may be hard 4 some and easy 4 others.
I'm thinking this person is more then just a piece of a$$ or my children's mother.

She's at a point where she doesn't even come
home anymore;
yet I have my head in the clouds telling friends and family that I love her.

We had come a long way from the days of walking each other 2 class
or cutting school
so a brotha could get some a$$.
Here I am and my heart is torn
4 I'm finding it very hard 2 move on.

It's like my mind is not seeing I'm slowly losing this person 2 who she calls just a friend. I
4gave her after the 1st time yet the same thing keeps happening again and again.

2 people can't speak at the same time—
some1 has 2 listen, yet there are a lot of fu3ken gaps
4 there were a lot of things I was just 2 blind 2c,
4 it's some other female/male she's kissin'.

The 1 who I would live and die 4
has become more like a whore.
It's 4 our children that I've stayed to this point rather then walking out the front door.

I'm slippin' not yet fallin'—
I need 2 get my sh!t on point,
4 the love that gave my heart life is gone.
Has me smoking a pack a day wondering where did I go wrong?
4 the spark that gave me life has moved on.

I'm at a point where I don't know
what 2 do or 2 feel.
If me smoking and drinking doesn't kill me fu3ken with this chick will.

Better Days

I recall the days of sleeping on park benches being deep in the trenches.
Out there without a care;
on a block pitching rock
not givin' a damn about the cops.

Sh!t scrambling, panhandling,
old dad out looking 4 a fix
not givin' a sh!t about me or my mom,
just that poison in his arm.

Mom out looting; grew up in an apartment that had rat's u can 4get mice!
Have my friends come over?
n!gger please don't believe the hype.

Lights might work, but not the heat,
may have heat yet lil' 2 eat.
Wearing other people's clothes—
2 poor 2 say no.
"No frills" was a household name.
As a child this kind of sh!t had me thinking I was the 1 2 blame.
Had me at the age young age of 10, wondering who the hell are these men
I keep seeing coming and going?
mom doing what she had 2
so I can get the new Puma's or Adidas 2 wear.
Teachers saying I'll never amount 2 sh!t
and how I need help.

No blue skies, no mama's apple pie, just me asking a God I couldn't see why? Why? Why?

Spending my days wanting something 2 eat,
so I spent less time at home
and more in the street.
At the age of 15 I'm out on my own,
feeling like I'm grown.
Guess that's what happens when ya parents are never home.

I walked around with a lil 22
in my no-name boots.
So b4 my stomach gots 2 touching my back again I was going 2 get me some loot.

(cont.)

Had all I could stand, had 2 grow up and B what I thought at the time was a man.
Had it with sticking my hands
in my pockets and coming up with lint;
trying 2 make sense of it all…
fu3k playing ball
I was on the grind striven 2 have some peace of mind, just looking 4 better days.

*"It was hard learning 2b a Man
When there was no Man there 2 Show me?
I had to grow past being born a Fatherless Child" Beloved Sha*

N!gger Please/Fatherless Child

N!gger please where were u when mama's water broke?
Out somewhere shootin' dope!
N!gger please, where was that a$$ when she brought me n2 this world?
out in the street layin' with some other girl.
N!gger please, I recall when I lived on Gates and Nostrand
and u stayed just up the block, never understood why your fake a$$ never came by;
N!gger please, u knew where I lived… u knew where I stayed,
while your a$$ lived on Heroin between Weed and Alcohol.
Damn pay phones were just 10 cents then, was it 2 much 2 call?
Growing up I heard how u were such a lady's man, a lover a pimp;
yet all that trickin' u never gave my mama 1 red cent.

N!gger please u aint' no pimp you're a wimp.
Spending all your time doin' line after line, never havin' money 4 me but always 4 coke.
U never had time 2 teach me how 2 ride a bike, 4 u were 2 busy hitting the pipe.
I recall me praying who would die 1st,
me from running wild or u from that sh!t
u pushed in your veins?
I have children and you're not around 2 watch them grow or even know their names.

N!gger please 2 this day I hate your guts,
u just don't know how many times I wanted 2 put 1 in ya melon 4 all the pain u caused and
the lies u were telling me and my mother.

N!gger please that's so fu3ked up how at your funeral I learn I got a sista' and a brotha',
who I don't know--
this is not the way love is supposed 2 go.

I promise 2b more of a father 2 my children then u have been 2 me.
I just need 2 get this off my chest n!gger please.

Incarcerated Scar Faces

I remember the days of court cases
and getting chased across roof tops
by the cops
and down fire escapes.
Seems like just yesterday a brotha
was flippin' weight
and taken trips out of state.

I done pushed everything from weed, dope, coke, hash 2 fake coach bags;
Sh!t please I did it all in the name of getting cash pardon me if I'm moving 2 fast.
Yet when it comes 2 my seeds not eating n!gger please,

I'd get in that a$$, turn water n2 wine,
kept 2 9's named Universal and Justice
sayin' FTP u devils can't touch this.

I recall doing things I can't 4get as well a lot of things I wish I could.
Livin' that life never turns out good.
I lost family and friends, loads of paper
and a nice condo.
I lived the life that many cats rap about yet they really don't know.

Oh please no I didn't say this just 2 blow smoke up ya a$$.
I drop this 4 that young brotha/sista who maybe out there moving a lil 2 fast,
oh I know sh!t is real in the field, I have no time 2 sugar coat anything,
I tell it like is.

Now I fast and build and no longer kill,
do things with my lil girl like playing house; strive 2 teach our 5 sons right from wrong,
be a better husband a father then my so-called father was 2 me and my mom
trust me locked in jail is not where we belong.

*There comes a times in a child's life where he or she may start 2 grow up 2 fast.
We as parents have 2 do our part 2 lead them in the right direction and
not the wrong.*
Beloved Sha

Vicky/Growing Up Fast

I once knew a girl by the name of Vicky; she had a cute face and an ok figure.
She was only 13 but hung with the older kids on the block; cuttin' school, drinkin'
and smokin' pot.

Vicky was out there havin' sex without protection, by the time she turned 14,
Vicky was pregnant.

Old dad in jail doing his 3rd bid and Vicky's crackhead mother was left 2 raise 6 kids--
when she's not in the street lookin' 4 a fix doin' whatever 2 get a hit.
Vicky's boosting and turning tricks 2 help make ends meet.
Mama brings home some no-good n!gger from off the street.
Vicky is about 7 months 2 weeks,
mother leaves her alone
with her no good boyfriend and his grimy cousin.

They both have their way with Vicky; saying 2 each other she sure looks pretty.

Vicky goes 2 wash their filth from off her,
as she looks in the mirror and realizes
she can't live like this.
She's havin' a baby now and
doesn't know who the daddy is;
Vicky breaks down and gives up *hope*, takes the belt from her bathrobe and makes a rope.
"Young Girl Found Dead Baby Lives,"
This was some wild sh!t I had 2 deal with
growing up as a kid.

*"As a young boy, I thought the only way 2 prove I was a man was 2 get money—
and so I got it, any way that I could. I had a girlfriend and children 2 feed, and the
bills weren't paying themselves so I hustled-- I flipped weight.   I was just a brotha'
on the grind.*

*After some years, and some losses I came 2 understand that
no material thing was worth missing my child's first step,
or not being there 4 their first word.*

*I realized that I lost more than I gained, when I was hustling on the block—
It was then that my favorite quote became:*

'My Clothes Might be Dirty, But my Hands are Clean'"

Beloved Sha

Truth B Told

Truth B told, that drug game is no joke.
So many of our youth are caught up in the drug game looking 2 make a name,
2 make some paper yet receiving nothing but hard times and hails of bullets…
and how could I 4get JAIL…

As a community, we must get involved,
but 1st that child's parents must do his or her part ,sh!t I know it's hard.
We are not the makers of the planes and ships that drop drugs n2 our streets.
Yet we as a people need 2 stop talking
and get off our knees,
4 the powers that B
don't give a damn about u or me.

Truth B told I fell victim 2 the drug game
and was in it deep.
I lost all that I had when
I got sent up the creek;
My lil' girlfriend, all my material things

and so-called friends along with my house.
The Feds didn't care about my family
and threw them out.

Truth B told I was a fool!
went from thinking I was super bad,
2 fighting everyday 2 keep some cat from raping my a$$.

So my new name became #25333083;
it took me a longtime 2 realize how I brought my children nothing
but years of shame mixed with pain.

U have no idea… like R. Kelly " if I could turn back the hands of time,"
I would have never got n2 the life of pushin' weight, doing crimes, bustin' nines.
I would strive 2b more righteous
as well as refined.
Truth B told, the drug game is not the way 2 go
so 2 all my lil' thugs take it from a man who knows.

Paper Chase

I can remember the days of sitting on 20's pockets full of money
Havin' all the honeys and
cat's wanting 2b my buddy.

Pushing up on blocks goin'
out of state, flipping weight ,
doing what I had 2 do 2 get that cake.

So move over Tony, Gotti, Nino it was all about me yo.
Sh!t the biggest lawyer couldn't keep me out of the paper
And when the Feds pushed up on me;
it wasn't about what I was doing—
it was about them not getting any cheddar.
I was 17 carrying 2 Berettas.

Livin' life like a dream.
When your on that paper chase
that a$$ will do anything.

Gats I busted them, whips I pushed them, if u were 2 try even thinking about stopping my
seeds from eating or my cash flow
that a$$ would stop breathing.

Sh!t is real in the field.
These youngsters have no idea.
They believe that sh!t they hear from want 2b thugs who just happen 2 have a record deal.

Well that was then and this is now;
I had 2 get up out that sh!t
and turn my life around.

This government is some cold motherfu3kers
1st time getting caught and that's your a$$.

u got a gun-- they have them 2 u have a vest they have those 2.
U push a lil dope they manufacture all this sh!t then sell it 2 u.

My Body

My body yearns, wanting, needing
2b touched.
What seems like years has only been days since this man was f#@!$.

I just want 2b loved is that asking 2 much?
Don't know about u, but as 4 me I'm suffering from sex on the brain…
don't know how 2 explain don't know where I should start, or where 2 end.

Ok here goes, my body yearns 2b touched this is 1 night pay-per-view isn't coming
through, with its watered down PG-13 suckin' and fake fu3kin'.
This brotha' needs some good, good lovin', some color me bad, let me smack that a$$ type
of sh!t.

I'm a step above being a freak;
I just know how 2b me,
not 1 trying 2b some1 I'm not,
my woman comes home we're going 2b rockin' until the police come knockin'.

Child please, I need sex like air 2 breathe;
no time 4 bull so who am I kidding I need some of my baby girl's puddin'.

I have been this way since birth.
Sh!t! This is the deal going 2 keep it real,
I miss the smell, taste, sound of my woman and the way she feels.

My body yearns 2b touched. Damn!
What am I 2 do?
I'm here all alone and she won't B home 4 hours.
My lower half is starting 2 say:
"obey your thirst, obey your thirst."
Damn I need a cold shower.

Around the time of this poem, I was at a point in my life where I was in love with a woman who wasn't in love with me, and I just need 2 open my eyes.
Beloved Sha

Conflicting Thoughts

In the beginning things were so sweet, as time went by u would no longer speak.
I lost weight, wouldn't eat, couldn't sleep;
trying 2 figure out was it something I did or something I said?
We slept in the same house,
but damn, in 2 different beds.

I have given u all of me mentally as well as physically, when I come 2 u 4 love;
u tell me not now your real busy.

I really thought u loved me, so like a fool I got your name tattooed on my neck.
Here it is 3 years down the line and I begin 2 notice a
slight change
how u started not coming home,
telling me some bullsh!t like oh u worked a double and I didn't have ya cell phone.

I would say 2 u: "love is there something we need 2 talk about?"
All I would get was "n!gger u need 2 stop."

Enough is enough, this so-called relationship has gone 2 hell.
Even friends and family could tell--that something was wrong.
Your twisted love had a brotha's head spinning.

Your a$$ just don't know how many nights I thought about sending u home.
Every other day some female or guy u work with calling our home.

These things u were doing were really messing up my head,
but not more than the day that I came 2 find out
some female and guy had been sharing our bed.

Don't Tell Me

Look, don't tell me u love me, but no longer show me.
Don't tell me u love me but can't recall when was the last time u held me in your arms.
Don't tell me u love me when u leave me all alone,
but when you're home if your not sleep you're on the Fu3ken phone.
Don't tell me u love me 4 when was the last time u put me b4 another?
Don't tell me u love me when it's u who has a secret lover--that is no secret 2 me.
U want 2 have your cake and eat it 2.
Damn girl I would really B a fool if I believe u love me and stay with u.
Don't tell me u love me, tell it 2 that other man/woman
I'll B the 1 smiling when he or her dumps you're a$$.
Don't come crying 2 me telling me u love me 4 I don't love u so don't tell me!

Why Me? Just When U Think U Know A Person

I placed my heart within your hand;
never wanting anything more than 2 love u and B your man.

How many times have u told me that I'm always on your mind?
How no other could ever take my place or my space…Why me?

4 it was your "friend" occupying all your time… Why me?

Where was this n!gger when u and your son had no heat or food 2 eat?
I'll tell u his a$$ was out running wild in the street.

I have been there 4 u when u were down in your luck, now I see why u stopped showing me and giving me love,
always telling me it's that time of the month,
treating me like I'm some kind of punk…
Why me?

Oh my brotha' I haven't 4gotten about u;
Yes I'm the same cat whose face u would smile in, then have the nerve 2 ask me if I wanted 2 kick it or shoot pool?

Now here the both of u stand thinking sh!t is sweet, u don't love me-- and trust me his a$$ doesn't love u!

(cont.)

Girl u could have told me rather then let find out like this.
I was blinded by a big a$$ and a smile, thinking it was love.
4 a long, long time I thought what took place was due 2 me, then I realized she was just a fallen angel who lost her wings
and needed 2b set free.
yet from time 2 time I ask myself, why me?

Sh!t Is Real

Yes sh!t is real in the field.
Babies making babies 4 he thinks it makes him a man;
Babies having babies 4 she just wants 2b loved,
yet nobody understands.

Sh!t is real! Corners are filled with dirty old men who do nothing
but drink cheap wine and talk about how they were the man back in the day.

Sh!t is real! Our youth are robbing and killing each other over bullsh!t colors,
nickels and dimes.
Even a blind person could see we as a people are facing some hard times.

Sh!t is real! Mothers turn tricks so that their seeds can have a hot meal
and a place 2 stay, as the powers that B do nothing but smile and say have a nice day.
She does all she can even though it's wrong, but 4 her it's the only way.
Affordable housing and good jobs are hard 2 find, so many of our people sitting home on
public assistance and the unemployment line.
Sh!t is real!

Burnt Out

I can't take it and I'm not the 1 2 fake it,
I find myself wondering more and more what is it all 4?
Would things B better if I just packed my sh!t and headed 4 the door?
Sh!t was sweet, Sh!t was fine, now all we do is argue all the time.
All she wants 2 do is party telling me it helps eases her mind.

I come across big a$$es and pretty faces everyday, but I'm not about 2 throw away years of being with a person
4 a roll in the hay.
Got sistas thinking I'm gay just because I wouldn't give them the time of day.

It will not B long b4 she'll have my a$$ going 2 court, yes u guessed it 4 child support.
Thank God during this hard a$$ time 4 pay-per-view, 4 it's been many cold nights that sh!t came through.

At 1time we were the best of friends, now we don't even speak;
she sleeps in our bed and I sleep on the couch with no covers, she's not given me sex
4 she has 3 or 4 different lovers.

She is doing her thing and it's
about time I start doing mine.
Like Boys 2 Men we have come
2 the end of the road,
Mama was so right when she said they'll B days like this.

Only God knows how I yearn 2b kissed or touched, just want a woman 2 love me 4 me.
I'm like damn just b a woman and stop lying 2 my a$$.
How many times can a person keep getting kicked in the a$$
b4 I realize I'm wasting my time?
So I think the best thing 2 do is not 2 fuss or 2 pout,
just pack my sh!t 4 I'm burnt out.

Damn Damn Damn

Well damn it's the same old song,
sh!t is still wrong.
Done went from the spark, addicted, burnt out 2 moving on.
My heart is torn who am I kidding? Who am I fooling? This is not where I belong.

Women are funny,1 minute they love u and the next they don't know u.
I loved this woman I thought I knew this woman; I got played by this woman damn!

I saw it coming, who wants 2b wrong?
When all I wanted was this woman in my life,
well 1st the sex stopped, then the conversation, now we both are moving on, but in 2
different directions.

She needs her space I just needed her,
how sh!t went wrong is 1 big blur.
Well damn! Her idea of a relationship
is not the same as mine.
4 She wants 2b free n party all the time.
Did I tell u I started smoking a pack a day?
Breaking my foot off in her a$$ is what I'm thinking yet I know if I do that
my next destination will B the police station. Damn!

Ok, ok, enough is enough. The situation had me being other then myself, smoking and drinking and that's just not me. So I got my head out of that cloud it had been in and realized I needed 2 move on. Beloved Sha

Moving On/Letting Go

Yes I'm moving on.
No more wondering what went wrong;
singing that same old sad song;
Am I hurt? Yes, but the break up has made me strong,
4 I have 2 move on.
I am now a better man, I understand.
Not sure what life has planned; but moving on 2 better and bigger things;
took off the ring now I can do my thing.
Thanks 4 opening my eyes, 4 now I see;
I can stop stressing over the things u did and think about me.
It's just the way things have 2b.
I can 4 the 1st time B truthful
when I say I'm happy.

Black Girl Lost

Black girl lost, walk that walk, talk that talk;
Continue 2 walk around with all ya a$$ out lookin' like a clown,
getting high, getting used.
You're a woman; a Blackwoman lost not looking 2B found.
All u care about is shaking ya a$$ allover town.
Black girl lost u went from a down earth sista 2 a low life b!tch,
may I ask u how long will it B b4 u start turning tricks?
Got ya nails done and oh a Nextel phone,
damn I see baby girl is all grown.
Black girl lost, when was the last time u kept you're a$$ home?
Black girl lost, who thinks she's the boss;
But I'm sorry love you're getting pimped by the very ones u think are your friends.

It's funny how I can see this
oh and so can others,
u gone with your new found lover
yes I'm talking 2 u.

I'm telling u what other don't,
what other so-called men and friends won't.
Black girl lost, don't feel bad when u land flat on your face,

just remember I told u 1st, 4 it's not your mind
they are after.
They just want 2 use u then they R off 2 the next or back 2 their X.

So after u have given this 1 and that 1 a taste ,and they don't come around,
just bend over and pick your face off the ground.
Black girl lost with, ya lil' press on nails, Nextel phone, and coach bag.
Ask yourself was loosing the only man who ever gave a damn
worth wanting 2b in the street?
Like my mama always said if ya lay down with dogs
u will get up with fleas.

Part II (Tears No More)

*And so I let go of the relationship
and moved on...
I had been with her since I was around 16, had been faithful, and given it my all and in
return I got her a$$ to kiss.
So I didn't want 2 love any woman, or feel anything.
I wasn't ready to be committed 2 anyone.
I decided 2 just breathe and "do me".*

Beloved Sha

Confession

Ok here goes, this man is about 2 come clean.
When it comes 2 obeying my thirst
I need that sh!t like air 2 breathe,
No minute man so ya best believe I got this,
have a virgin's sh!t drippen with just 1 kiss.

N2 hours of crushen' in all positions and pullen' ya hair, love scratches on my back, hitten it from the rear.

Hickeys on my neck and going home with ya thong. Now u do recall me saying I was in a class by myself when it comes 2 crushen?
Ok just checken, my lower half stays
in the up ward direction.

This man always packs protection,
have that a$$ thinken' she'
s on a stairway 2 heaven.
I'm just being real 4 no I'm not playen',
Know this is not just hype I'll have that a$$ not walken' right.
I just had 2 take a minute and come clean u know us Gemini's we like sh!t in pairs and are down 4 anything.

Insatiable

Oh don't get me wrong, never feel like your being disrespected or ever feeling neglected.
What's that u say?
u got hit with the unexpected?
love I strive 4 nothing but perfection.
Close ya eyes and enjoy this
subliminal erection.

No need 2 worry this brotha' has protection. As u see I'm not your average size brotha',
lay back baby and enjoy hours and hours
of oh so good lovin'.
This is possible boo 4 I'm "Insatiable"
so with that being said;
lights, camera, action--nothing but pure satisfaction.

I Slipped

I Slipped. Nobody will ever believe this crazy sh!t, I was on my way 2 the Apollo on the A train when I ran n2 2 dime pieces that were given me the eye, oh yes they were fly.

1 said she liked my suit ,
the other hugged me rubbing her chest up on me as I said thank u. Both looking cute.
I slipped now from the vibe I was picking up on these 2 wanted 2 get it on looking 4 some action these females had no idea how I would give them both supreme satisfaction.
As I reached in my back pocket just 2 make sure I had my XL Magnum.

I Slipped. The convo went from what I'm doing 2 where I'm going?
Sh!t was just flowing .
Baby girl who complimented me on my suit had slid my hand between her thighs without me knowing.

At this point I knew I wasn't going 2 the Apollo, here is when they talk amongst themselves then said let's get of here, and go 2 a hotel? I slipped.
It took a minute 2c they were not playing 4 in a minute I would B all in it.

I Slipped. We get 2 the telly Cindy ties my hand as Shelly gets a blind fold out her bag,.
At this point I'm like I'm down 4 whatever.
Cindy pulls out a gun and robs a brotha
4 all my jewels,
takes my black Kenneth Cole watch
and the matching shoes.
Damn I slipped that was the summer I believe of 86 when I slipped see what happen when a man is thinking with his d!3k.

Not all Men

What is it about some men that have some women thinking we're all the same?
Is it that we all cheat, beat our women
and can spit game?
Or is it that all men do nothing but drink, smoke, play video games and know how 2 call women b9tches rather then their name?

What is it about some men that have some women thinking we're the 1 2 blame?
Like when sh!t gets tough all men breakout because we can't stand the rain.
What is it with some (and in no way am I calling any1 dumb) women rather blame men 4 fallen short and not showing support?

Now I don't mean 2 get any1 mad,
but not all men are like the last so-called man you might have had;
who don't care of their children
or get a kick out of whipping a women's a$$.

What is it with some women who seem 2 think
a man wants get between their thighs, Just because he speaks.
Or that if she doesn't speak, every man will call
you b!tches, tricks, mud kicker and whores.
Or that all men love being in the street, getting pissed off because their shirt is not ironed or u didn't fix them anything2 eat.

On behalf of us 100% real men who know how 2 cook and clean,
who know how 2 treat a woman like a queen,
know that not every man falls weak 2 a big butt and a smile and just because we may look or say hi; it doesn't mean we're looking 2 get between your thighs.

Not all men fall short in showing a woman support, 4 a real man would raise the next so-called man's child like it's his own, and
give his woman the coat off his back if she gets cold.

(cont.)

A real man would rather talk than fight,
a real man is 2 busy making sure the bills are paid,2 B thinking about damn video games.
A real man wouldn't need 2 drink or get high; a real man would only need 2 look in his woman eyes.

I'm an upright man and
when I speak I shine.
I don't scratch where I don't itch;
happy as hell with the woman I'm with,
who has 2 much respect 2 call a woman a b9tch.
So baby girl baby please don't ever get it twisted in thinking all men are the same;
just know I'm real with my sh!t so who needs 2 spit game?

How Many

Dear God how many wrongs do I have 2 make b4 something goes right?
The same kind of women keep coming into my life.
1 starting 2 show me she's crazy,
has the nerve 2b telling people we're having a baby.

Then there's the 1 who every other day wants some1 new in her life,
yet when his or her a$$ wasn't around they'd call me 2 make things right.

Had me doing stuff like make sure the kids got off 4 school, clothes get washed,
and if I was good I might get some sex at the end of the night.

Then there's the 1 who seems 2 know
how 2 get me mad,
can't lie we crushed a few times then this fool goes out and gets my name tattooed on her a$$.

Some men would B glad 2 have a woman that went both ways;
I just wanted a woman whose love was here 2 stay and didn't play games.

(cont.)

Not here 1 minute then gone the next,
Sh!t wasn't right just because she gave me a lil sex.
OK who's next?

Now as I was saying then there's this girl who thinks I'm playin.
I have a mother and I don't need another.
Coming with this who was that?
What am I doing?
Where have I been? With who?
And why not get married?
That sh!t God I'm just not havin',
I have a question can I just breathe?
Can I live?
Why the hell must a person B so
Over-protective;
and always looking at things so damn negative?
Talk 2 me God 4 something has 2 give!

Reality
(An Answer to Chocolatepeach)

So love is that right u relinquish all control?
Are you really mines, meaning mind body and soul?
Damn if so what a rush.
This man craves your touch.

U may lie within my embrace now and always never looking back just 4wards.
Everyday and night feeling exhausted pleased and weak in the knees, no need 2 tease.

This is not a fantasy this is reality your moans and cries are music 2 my ears.
As I hold u close 2 me in lick your tears, never fear 4 the true and living superman is here.
Love u want 2 explode then by all means lay back and go 4 what u know.

Damn baby hurt me hurt me! No I'm not your average brotha just a damn good lover.
Loven u from the top of your head down 2 your feet,
what's that u say? U can't speak?

No need. I can hear your thoughts.
within my love u shall lose all track of time,
know that when I tap that a$$ that a$$ is indeed mine,
know this baby girl I don't justmake love 2 your body
I make love 2 your mind.

So how does it feel? U can tell by the look on my face in the hickeys on ya neck,
as I slowly kiss ya nipples and play with ya cl*t.
Always given u pleasure with a lil pain
Sprinkle me baby with that candy rain as u call my name.
If u ask me I think you're a bad girl trying 2b good not a good girl trying 2b bad;
but if u say so turn around so I can spank that thick a$$.

*OK so now I'm single yet I'm slowly learning even
being single wasn't drama free...*
Beloved Sha

P.M.S.N
Now I don't know what the deal is
old girl is bugging,
baby girl is stressing
her a$$ acts like she is P.M.S.N

I minute she's hot 1 minute she's cold 1 minute she doesn't need a brotha,
the next she's like why won't u hold me?
she's P.M.S.N

I know they say "if it aint' rough it aint' right"
can't take the bullsh!t 2 tired 2 fight.
I can do without the drama in my life.
Girl is fine though sh!t is a lil crazy 4 its fu3ken with my mind.

She just acts like she's on a 24 hour period
all the time.
She's P.M.S.N but it's my nerves she's testing, a brotha started smoking!
and no I'm not joking;!
shorty acts real funny when it comes 2 given up the booty, has the nerve 2 say I'm moody.
She's P.M.S.N

Suicidal Thoughts P2

These thoughts of suicide are more then I can bear.
When I attempt 2 open up 2 others,
they seem as if they don't care,
So at this point I just rely on self-- truth B told I need help,
People telling my I look like my mother but act like my father.
Please! my father was a nobody putting all kinds of sh!t in his arm;
plus he was never around.
Crazy how I can't remember his face,
but can recall his name.
Suicidal thoughts, ya know a man can't stand on 1 legfeel more and more
like I wish I was dead.

The sh!t I deal with every day is killing me if it wasn't 4 my children I'd take a dirt nap;
push my sh!t way back.

When I look n2 their eyes they touch a part of me that keeps me alive.
I'm feeling like I can't breathe;
got a lot of sh!t on my mind.
If it wasn't 4 them pop, pop goes the 9.

Suicidal thoughts, yet then they would B without a father 4 they don't have a mother,
she ran off with her new found lover.

Suicidal thoughts right now times are hard and paper is tight,back against the fall got's 2
stand tall ,have 2b there 4 my children.
It's more than my so-called father gave me;
which was nothing but a lot of broken promises and pipe dreams.
U know it felt good 2 get that off my chest suicidal thoughts have now been put 2 rest.

Brown Eyes

Girl was fine girl was thick in the thighs had a pair of deep brown eyes,
every now and then she would peep at a brotha when I'm pulling in or out my house.

Bumped n2 her at a party on the island
I was with my girl so
I didn't think it would B a problem,
I was at the bar listening 2 Sade…
or was it India Arie?

Anyway girl slid me a drink and said some crazy sh!t like
"u seem like a brotha who thinks."
Now what do I do? She seems 2b disrespecting my baby, and she was out of line.
I'm going 2b real girl was fine
yet here is where I had 2 let her know
She was wasting her time.

It's not a crime 4 people 2 people speak,
yet baby girl knew I had a lady 4 she lived right up the street.

I played it smooth told her thanks 4 the drink and kept it moving now here comes my baby
who says
"oh so u know each other?"
I step out side 2 get some air who do u think I bumped n2 wearing just a rain coat and no
underwear ? Gave me her # tells me she wants 2b my lil secret lover.

This chick her must of thought I was stupid,
given my the # and address 2 her place,
I did what any real man would of done-- and threw the drink in her face.
"I've got a woman so what do I need u 4?"
A$$ looking dumb as her mouth hit the floor.
This is what I left thinking about b4 I walked out the door.
News flash I have a woman I think with my brain and not my d!ck
and you wonder why some people call u a b9tch.

I'm at the point where getting back in the game is not a question, and being with a no good female has my head spinning in like a million directions, I'm just looking 4 a good woman, 1 I can know that's all mine. I keep telling myself things will be better this time, yes this time...

Beloved Sha

A Good Woman

A good woman is hard 2 find.
we as men should love a woman 4 more then just a big a$$ and acknowledge
they do have a mind.
A good woman can B looking u right in the face, but a lot of men worry about what's on
the next mans plate.

A good woman could B what some call fat, thick, slim, short or tall;
a good woman is 1 who will stand by her man and not let him fall.
A good woman is more than 1 who can take care of bi in the bedroom,
but sh!t the boardroom as well as the kitchen;
1 who knows how 2 speak her mind as well as
Listen.

A good woman could B the girl next door
or the 1 scrubbing Burger King floors,

We as men must stop treating our women like a sex toy and if she is 2 slip we as men must
help pick her up.

We as men must weed out all the bullsh!t and mud kickers that clouds our minds.
Put aside the big a$$, cute face and the bling, bling; the whip she drives, if she has kids,
and if she makes more then we do;
and see the Blackwoman 4 who she is-- God's most precious jewel.

Drama

Who needs drama is the question I like 2 ask?
Whatever happen 2 the days of just chillin' with that special some1
and at the end of the night get a lil a$$.

Drama is something every1 can do with out it's the bullsh!t that just makes even the
strongest person stop saying no and want 2 punch a person in the mouth.

No let me stop playin I'm just keeping it real,
it's the bullsh!t drama u know the baby daddy/baby mama,
where were u last night drama?

The sh!t that just keeps on eatin' at u and u start feelen like damn!
What do I do? 2 the point u look at he or her and say n!gger/b9tch u know what fu3k u!!!
When some mother#@$! just don't know how 2 let another B happy!
U know damn! Can a mother@#$!! breathe?

Coming with that bullsh!t child please!
I'm not a crash dummy, this sh!t here is far from funny, we all go through this sh!t
some 2, 3 times a day being or just knowing some people the price u pay.

Right about now I'm ready 2 change my name keep my sh!t in my pants!
Who me? No way, not ready to be celibate and I'm damn sure not gay;
I can't go that route.

I love my beautiful Black sistas,
it's the drama I can do without like the
where were u? Who is that?
Why can't I come over?
When I pay the f*3ken bills in my own house.

Drama, I don't have a P.O. your not my C.O or warden.
I just want the 1 with whom I can chill and grow old.

Days/nights full of good, good lovin',
so 2 all those females/males stop with the buggin'.
This goes out 2 my brothas 2 stop with the bullsh!t b4 your left with just ya d!ck in your
hand, comin' with that "yo baby, baby please, baby understand".
I 2b drama free sh!t this way 1 of us will B happy.

Let's Not Get It Twisted/I'm Not Them

Let me just get this off my chest,
no baby girl please,
I'm not the last man or previous cats who treated u like a door mat.

Let's not get it twisted after placing heaven at their feet yet they choice 2 creep,
Yet a man such as self could never B within that category.

See I love you mind, body and soul;
u just choose 2 keep holding on 2 the things other men who were in your life did to u
and that sh!t has 2 stop.

Let's not get it twisted I'm a man understand
I'm not about 2 back down 2 any cat out there,
what I tell u goes in 1 ear and out the other, I'm a real man so who needs a secret lover?
Being 2gether doesn't me we're connected at the hip or the minute things get a lil rough I
gots 2 get with the next chick.

Let's not get it twisted I'm not those lames u know their names, who just wanted the a$$ 4
I'm in a class by myself;
if this man came in the form of a drink--
truth B told I'd B top shelf.
Love I know u been hurt I know u been burnt by other b4 me who couldn't see or know
what they had.

Dear, let me clear the air,
I have had my share as well.
Let's not get it twisted these weak a$$ men really did a # on your heart and head,
know I'm not 1 2b jumping from bed 2 bed I feel your pain, I feel your sorrow know this
the love u push away 2day,
may not B here tomorrow.
Let's not get it twisted.

The Rabbit Died

The rabbit died u have 2 pardon a brotha' 4 I don't usually talk this way, but this b9tch lied; had a brotha feeling all messed up inside;
now in the back of my mind I'm like shorty is playing me, can't fall 4 what she's telling me.

Understand now when I got with her she was a lil chubby around the stomach, yet I paid it no mind I'm man enough 2 say;
I was 2 busy thinking about waxing that behind,
The rabbit died.

Ok 2 make a long story short I layed it down;
not 2b funny yet trust and believe I put it down flipping her a$$ in every direction
what's so funny was I always used protection.
I had 2 take a minute and ask myself well how in the hell did she get pregnant?
I had 2 do the math couldn't let myself get sidetracked by a piece of a$$,
the rabbit died.

Now I only knew her 4 a minute
had 2 think of who else may have been hitting it, this here was no joke,
the condom never broke;

I never hit it raw start asking myself maybe she was playing u from the door?

Had me counting the times we crushed,
started wondering could girl B a lil touched.
Now I didn't have much yet I had my sh!t 2getherthis girl starts saying this sh!t 2 the next woman I was with and then to my mother.

Now my moms hitting me on the cell like Beloved what's the deal?
Mom come on here B 4real, her havin' my baby? Please, ain't no, ifs, ands, or maybes; girl is just damn crazy.

Truth B told she was doing this sh!t because she wants 2 know why I left her
I need 2b with no female who wants 2 tell me where I'm going or when I can go see my own children or kick it with my brotha,
girl must have been smoking.
About 2 weeks later I get the strangest email telling me "oh Beloved I'm sorry," her telling me she was having a baby was just 2 keep me there, the rabbit died yea, yea, yea.

Here I am striving 2 get over the bull from the drama and stress of what seems like ever chick I come across pray to God let me fine Mrs. Right for I know shes out there.
                                    Beloved Sha

Can I?

Can I find a real woman
that will love me just 4 me?
1 that will mean she loves me
when she tells me,
so when I open myself 2 her
I will not feel like I'm wasting my time.

Can I find a woman who is understanding of my feelings as well as deepest needs and not
so important wants? Can I find a sista' who will make me feel like a king
and her my queen?
1 who will know within her heart I'm her everything, 4 she is mine;
Can I find a woman who
I can't just stop talking about,
who makes me hot all over? 1 who brings closure 2 this brothas' life,
1 that is happy 2b loved by this man and shows it in every way.
1 that will make my day as well as my night,
1 that will just love me and
never want 2 fuss or fight
Can I?

No, the question should B "when " will I find the woman who will 1day come n2 my life?
4 this man no longer wants 2b alone at night.

*So I'm still getting over a broken heart and I'm
Just doin' me and not looking 4 a love connection, yet knowing being alone is not where I want 2b. Now I'm at a point where I'm not chasin' women yet I have my choice of a number of them, when I find myself wanting and needing 2b with a woman who has been a friend since sh!t with my ex went 2 hell, I'm starting 2 realize I love her and I'm wondering can she tell.*
Beloved Sha

Cross The Line P1

Damn I think I did it this time, I know a young lady who I can't get off my mind.
Things keep going the way they are and I'll have 2 cross the line.
Damn God knows if I do that a$$ is mine.
Shortly is thick-with-it, Chocolate is fine;
not only does she have a nice a$$ this woman has a mind.
We vibe online and on the phone 4 hours,
girl has me getting off needing a cold shower.
\I'm feelin' baby girl in the worst way,
just hearing from her makes my day.
We have only known each other 4 a short time, but damn!
Even she is thinking about crossin' the line.

Right now we're friends, but the door is open 2b so much more.
When we speak we are very blunt, we tell each other what we need and want.
Baby girl tells me I'm in a class by myself and that I have mad game,
truth B told I get up in that a$$ and I'm given the keys 2 my heart as well as my last name
Chocolate will never B the same.
We have been blessed 2 become such friends and could even B great lovers,
if allowed the proper time,
but 4 now her and I are just friends takin' it
s-l-o-w
seeing who will be the 1st 2 cross the line.

So as it turns out baby girl was lovin a brotha 2, yet she had been hurt in the past and was afraid so we took things slow, just getting 2 really know each other b4 any1 crossed the line.
Beloved Sha

Just A Minute

Peace Blackwoman can I have a minute of your time?
No I'm not 1 of those cat's who try 2 pick a sista up with bullsh!t 1 lines,
I can get past the phat a$$
and see u do have a mind.

Just a minute Blackwoman my words are sincere, may I B the Blackman
who whispers sweet things in your ear?

just a minute love oh pardon me my name is "Beloved"
and yours might B? Its' got 2b Beautiful, Heavenly, Gods Precious Jewel,
4 me 2 call u Shorty, Chicken Head or B9tch would B playing myself.

Just a minute Blackwoman can I help it if I'm just the Blackman my mother raised me 2b?

Just a minute I must keep it real and tell u it's not easy being the man that I am;
when there are so many so-called men who don't give a damn and treat women like dirt!
Truth B told real men cry and get hurt.
I'm nothing like these cats u see standing on the corner undressing u with their eyes;
Just a minute u see small minds think small big minds think great,
so am I man enough 4 u love?
I think so, I'll call u about 8.

I'm Twisted

This woman has me twisted, no I'm not joking,
the sh!t she put on me has this brotha smoking,
she has become the weed 2 my " get high" the smoke in my "ci"
has me looking 4 her in the daytime with a flash light!
This woman is not just in my head, but damn she has my heart.
I don't remember the last time I felt like this;
I'm man enough 2 say baby girl has me whipped.
Her mental is deep her physical causes the strongest man 2 fall weak,
she gives me all I need and want so un-like most weak men I have no need 2 creep.
I've been around the block 2 many times
heard all the bullsh!t lines;
it's this woman I can't get off my mind;
bottom line I'm twisted.

Diamond In The Rough

I know many times b4 my heart has lied,
but in this day and time this brotha' needs a piece of mind,
some1 who is all mine; and never having 2 wonder is she's mine.
Who doesn't run lines and at the drop of a dime, is there when I call, there 4 me if I am 2
ever slip or fall.

Her and I being friends 4 eternity,
yet realizing just what I mean 2 her
hat she means 2 me.
Never going 2 bed mad, yet in each others arms feeling happy.

Sayin' lil' things like:
"honey, love, baby I got this pour u a glass of wine; let me get u something 2 eat."
It doesn't matter if she is
from the projects or the suburbs;
What matters is that she knows I love her.
So Blackwoman please 4give sweaty hands,
by all means know that b4 u stands a man.

I see u 4 more then a cute face and a big booty
A blind man could see you're beautiful.
Know this Chocolate, not just 4 your outer beauty your inner beauty,
I must say how your divine love soothes me as well as moves me.

Blackwoman know that these are not just lines, I just choose 2 share with u
what's on my mind; and may u come 2 find I love u and can't breathe without u.
Chocolate u cause me 2 never 4get just how good love is and how good it can B.
When I look at u I see the best part of me.
Your arms have always kept me safe when things went wrong; your lips enlighten me with
your wisdom and charm.

As I look within your deep brown eyes I see u never looking down on me yet lovin' me;
not 4 who I was, but 4 who I am; and not 4 what others want me 2b.

It is within your womb I see us giving birth 2 the universe, I thirst 2 drink and breathe in
your love; as we grow old 2gether and give names 2 each star and cloud.

Damn I love u so much going 2 s l o w it down 4 as u can see I'm talking a lil 2 much.
Just know Blackwoman, you're a diamond in the rough.

Line Crossed P2

Your love is so intoxicating the things u say 2 me so stimulating,
this is no bullsh!t baby; u'll B the death of me I know how this may sound,
but if I was blind your beauty I'd still see.
Love is 2 small of a word 2 define just what u mean 2 me.

Damn baby ya incredible, un4getable,
no I'm not playin',
u make a man want 2 get up out the game,
drop like 4 g's on a ring and bless u with his last name.

Ya' lips are sweet your tongue is divine,
b4 I had such a woman as ya self u only existed in my mind. Baby u give me feva!
Got a brotha willing 2 cut your grass,
wishing I was the bubbles in your bath.

May I B the voice when its no1 there,
u can count on me
even if it's just 2 lend an ear.
May I B the 1 who's name u write in the sand;
telling the world I'm your man, may I B the only 1 2 ever place a ring on your hand.

I no longer want 2 fight the feeling of not crossing the line. I made up my mind that a$$
is mine!

Tongue Tied

I met this woman and God I can't lie,
this woman has done something 2 me which leaves me tongue tied.

I've started noticing how I can't eat or sleep how when I'm around her my legs get weak.
Going 2 put it out there and tell ya there's no sex sweeter.

Sh!t I'm going 2b real can't wait 2 eat her;
she has me open with those soft lips and thighs, she really put something on me that has me tongue tied.

Not only is she beautiful,
the woman has a mind;
she's 1 of the deepest sistas I've come 2 know in a long time.
She has me feeling like I'm whipped 2 the point there's so much I want 2 show her and
say… but I don't want 2 rush her or
push her away.

Baby girl has shown and proved 2b able 2 make my days as well as my nights,
if she keeps this up girl will b my wife,
I have 2 stop denying myself the love she gives and the joy she brings and come clean.

I'm tongue tied I've been here b4;
but something about this woman that telling me she's the 1;
I can't recall when I've felt so loved and had so much fun.

Thinking of U

The tears in my eyes burn, I yearn 4 your touch,
u have me feeling like I'm 15 again, 4 I'm going nuts ready 2 bust.
Damn! U and I makin' moves is cool 4 we have 2 eat
and get that $$$ "cream" cash rules everything around me.
Me wanting the Jag and u wanting that Lex or the Benz jeep;
Sh!t! I haven't seen u in weeks yet I remain strong
Now I might look, but I don't creep;
I pull out your picture when I'm feeling weak.

U know the 1 u of your chocolate thighs, beautiful brown eyes,
luscious lips and heart shaped a$$.
As u can see this brotha' has it bad
Pay-per-view can't help me with this sh!t.

It's my Chocolate Sunday I miss, sh!t!
From Sunday- Saturday I know I sound spoiled
I just want 2 lay with you and plant my seeds within your fertile soil.

My baby is not lazy or just doesn't care,
She and I are just makin' moves so we can have that house with 3 baths,
a pool, 2 car garage and 8 bedrooms.
I with my book and clothing line her with her own BI.
Sometimes we just don't have the time.

So we do silly stuff like play phone tag, or hitting the 2way.
If u think I'd give her up 4 any chick out there I beg your pardon not now days.
4 I could never find another who makes me feel like this,
just want her 2 know if ya didn't know I love u well I do from the bottom of my heart I'll
do all in my power 2 show and prove my love is true, at all times protecting u and
respecting u as the queen u are.

Where I Want 2b/ Should B

Baby know I'm sorry 4 the stuff I put u through,
I was going through a lot of changes and couldn't see
yet trying 2 play cool and keep my own sh!t 2gether.
Over the course of time 3 years I have wrote u a bunch of cards and letters…
yet they were never mailed.
Right now I have 2 come clean and clear the air.
A love such as yours is very rare.
Even though I seemed happy things all around me were falling apart
on my end of the square.
Beautiful u have no idea how I wanted 2 just jump on a bus, plain or train
so we could B in the same place locked in a bonded kiss our bodies wet from sweat as we
become 1 breathing in each others love until the sun comes out.

In the back of my mind my heart always knew
if I couldn't have u sh!t then I didn't want any1,
we have come so far from being friends 2 being more then lovers,
we even think the very same things.
It will not B long b4 we are looking at his and her rings,
so please know where u are is where I want 2b and should B 4 there's nothing keeping me
here in New York, I just want 2 love u unconditionally.

New Birth

Blackwoman, I need u in my life more then air 2 breathe.
U have a brotha ready
2 get down on 1 knee.
I look at u and u know what I see?
I see the best part of me, my other half;
us drying each other tears.
U and I sharing bubble baths, yet baby girl that's just the half.
Here b4 u stands a man who looks past
the big butt, thick thighs, and deep brown eyes.
A long time ago I came 2 realize u are
without a doubt my other half.
There are not enough hours in a day 2 let u know what I feel.

What's havin' a house if it's not a home?
What's the point in havin' friends if it's u who put and end 2 the Blackman being alone?
Got a brotha phone set 2 his & her ring tones.

Blackwoman my Fertile earth,
at 1 time I told u:
"As I step out of all that I'm wearing n2 the darkness, I close my eyes
and become wet within your love.

Truth B told your smile is as warm as a hug on
a cold day, damn Chocolate I need a hit of that 4 you're my drug and I see
I truly have an addiction.
What I make known is an actual fact not fiction.

Well at this point he and I are talking like 3, 4, 5 times a day when our 2 hearts become 1. Leaving the pain of our past relationships and strive 2 build on 1 that we are more then sure will out last time our love 4 each other is divine.

Beloved Sha

The Dawn Of Creation

Cocooned in a warm blanket of darkness,
the Blackman brings 4th life,
giving light 2 the universe sparked from a kiss and the movement of your thick hips.

As I travel within your deep black hole as u ride my cosmic milky way,
with no delay I stimulate your body as well as your mind.

This magnetic steaming hot sun is far from done, 4 there is only 1 sun such as self;
so give in as your knees get weak from this Blackman's touch.

The dawn of creation; now tell me you don't feel my divine love circulating.
Not 1 2 procrastinate; u can call it the mysteries of the heavens or just call it fate.

When our physical forms pass I shall B waiting at heavens gate,
contemplating the possibility of relinquishing your physical form,
as we become 1 with the atoms and swirl into one another's direction.
Black woman enjoy the mental erection.

Do understand what I'm saying 4 no love I'm not playing.
The dawn of creation, by all means do the knowledge 2 what I'm saying.
No time 4 the bullsh!t so Blackwoman let's do this.

I love the way u smell, taste, and feel my Nubian queen I'm just keeping it real.
So as I lay between your thighs enjoying the dawn of creation,
know Blackwoman you bring this man more than peace of mind.

Hot All Over 4 Fertile

Damn! The other morning this sista introduced me 2 the love of a life time.
Now I'm hot all over, she put it on me yes she did, this way and that way;
had a brotha' spelling (can u believe!?)
her name?

My new -found queen, now I'm hot all over.
If only every morning, afternoon and night could B like this.
Oh damn!
The way she held me and kissed me with those soft sweet lips,
nibbling on a brotha's neck and sh!t.

1st sista' 2 have my head in the clouds,
man enough 2 tell ya she had me calling and spelling her name out loud.

Haven't felt like this in sometime can't get this sista off my mind. Keep telling her:
"baby damn do that thing u do 1more time."
We kissed as we both went 2 rest on our bedroom floor, had 2 come clean and tell my
woman ya man's sh!t is sore, now I'm hot all over 4 Fertile.

Hell Of A Woman

I close my eyes, I dream of u;
I imagine the taste of your lips the feel of your hands and mine, and the softness of your
hair brushing against my face
then suddenly I'm feeling strong yet weak from my need 4 u Blackwoman.

When u hold me close, then look n2 my eyes as u whisper how much u love me.
I'm carried gently 2 another place, your love awakes me feel so alive and proud of the
Blackwoman that u are.

Yet when the stairs fade and the sun shines in our window u kiss me, I awaken needing u
even more then I did the day b4.
I'm missing u badly Blackwoman,
I wish u were here.

Though your far away in my heart u'll stay, I'll only 2 dream about u Blackwoman and I
escape 2 a that place in my heart,
where we're never apart
my amazing Blackwoman.

Can't Breathe Without U

Can't breathe without u Blackwoman.
Your love is intoxicating
your touch is so stimulating.
I don't just dream about you, it's as if thoughts of you Blackwoman
bring heaven 2 the king's every waking hour.

Can't breathe without u;
The warmth of your thighs puts a smile on my face. there's no other place
I'd rather be then with u baby.

Can't breathe without u;
I more than need your love I hunger 4 it;
the way a man doing life craves a hot baths, freedom, sunshine and a good woman.

Can't breathe without u;
I'm more than in love with u Blackwoman.
I'll do all within my power 2 show and prove my love is true.
At all times protecting u and respecting u as the queen u are.

I'm open 4 your love, Blackwoman,
you're the best part of me,
can't breathe with out u;
this man needs u like air 2 breathe.

What?

What is it about u
that always causes me 2 smile?
Could it b the sexy look within your eyes?
What is it about u that has me feeling like I can't get enough?

What is it about u
that has me longing 4 your touch?
What is it about u that has me all choked up?
What is it about u that has me not wanting 2 fuℂk, but rather make love?

Well I'll tell u, it's more then your eyes that look at me each night.
It's more then your arms that hold me tight.
It's more then your thick a$$ I love 2 hold.
Chocolate,
what has me feeling this way,
is the thought of u and I growing old
2gether some day.

If God Was A Woman

If God was a woman she would
have style and grace,
a tight a$$ figure and a pretty face.
Soft skin, no weave, or fake a$$ nails,
4 everything about her would B real.

If God was a woman-- yes I know this sounds crazy, she would let men know what's it's
like 2 have cramps and 2 have a baby.

If God was a woman she would have a supreme mind and no woman would B looked at as
just a "dime."
4 on a scale of 1-10 she would B a "12",
put your hands on a woman,
your a$$ is going 2 hell 4get jail.

If God was a woman,
no disrespect, and don't get me wrong,
her sexy a$$ would B wearing a thong.
She would educate women who go around half dressed on how 2 keep their legs closed,
and make sure all men know that
no means no!

If God was a woman the penalty
4 rape would B death,
not claimin' your children would carry life,
and there would B a law:
"get ya balls cut off if u cheat on your woman, girl, or wife".

If God was a woman she would B 1 with the earth and man being 1 with the sun,
there would B no more drugs, crime, war or need 4 guns.

If God was a woman there would B more then just May 12th 2 honor mothers.
Men would have 365 days
2 show her they love her.

If God was a woman she would make things better, all nations would B able 2 live 2gether.
If God was a woman men wouldn't get away with a lot of the dumb sh!t we do.
We would love u more, respect u more, protect u more; do all within our power
2 let u know Blackwoman it's u we adore....
If God was a woman.

Chocolate Sunday

May I have a Chocolate Sunday please?
1 with lots of sprinkles and that real good whipped cream.
A double scoop of love that always has this man not knowing how 2 act,
b4 I get 2 the last scoop
has this man running back.

Oh and also some of that Chocolate syrup,
I've been thinking about her-- I mean it,
this all damn day,
my Chocolate Sunday is soft
and sweet 2 the lips.
I've always dreamed of this.

U just don't know, my Chocolate Sunday I could enjoy u 4 days,
I think the 1st time I had u
I was in the 3rd grade.
U can keep the nuts this right here
will B just fine,
my Chocolate Sunday I miss u baby you're always on my mind.

All That U Need

I am all that u need, and all that u shall ever want a Blackman 2b.
With age comes wisdom and with time comes change.

Blackwoman I am no longer other than myself, but I am what the Supreme Being created me 2b.

I am all that u need 4 in doing the knowledge 2 myself I came 2 understand
Black is beautiful.
Yes, the praises are due 2 the Blackman,
yet where would I B if not 4 the Blackwoman?

I am all that u need, I am an intelligent Blackman who stands strong on his square
4 looking deep within self I came 2 realize I am the square.
Black woman let it B understood that I place no limitation on u or the love that I have 4u.

I am all that u need, may u take my hand in the uplifting of our people
4 we are not the builders of tanks and bombs
and as we strive 2 rebuild city blocks and educate these babies
know within my eye u are my 1st lady.

I am all that u need, a Blackman who can create not just your deepest desire,
but take u 2 new levels mentally as well as physically.
I am all that u need Blackwoman,
I will now and always respect the foundation of the Black Family.

Blackwoman as you pursue your quest 4 mental growth,
I shall not feel threatened.
I will encourage u.

I am all that u need, may I B that shoulder u cry on, your Black Knight that will protect u
from the many demons that try 2 consume our peoples' minds and fertile soil daily.
May u B there 4 me if I am 2 ever slip or fall.

I am all that u need Blackwoman from out of the darkness I was brought n2 existence,
no longer a child, but a strong Blackman.
My refined queen I am all that u need,
4 I am the 1 your Beloved Blackman.

I Promise

Blackwoman until I meet u my greatest fear was never letting go;
It is your love 4 this Blackman that gives me strength.
I promise, Blackwoman that your love is the air I breathe,
truth B told you're the best part of me.
Blackwoman you're the part that makes me whole;
it's your love that keeps me warm,
a woman such as yourself is always on my mind.
Beautiful, your love is divine,
I promise, place your hand within my hand and we shall never part,
4 this Blackman is lovin' u with all his heart.
No matter how crazy things may get we shall never part.
I promise your love is the love that feeds my soul,
no1 but you love that I strive 2 have and 2 hold.
Within your love do I plan 2 make my home.
From our love we shall bring our dreams 2 life.

*Everyday as I look the news or read the paper how many of our
children are being lost to the street dead or in jail. No longer am
I the person your read about or the one that has your child pushen dope out of your
house..... To be blunt I grew up and woke up and I owe it all to that special lady in my life
and our children for I am indeed a changed man.* Beloved Sha

Changed Man

Ya know life seems so much better since a brotha is liven legal,
just thinking of how I'm a changed man;
I lived a hell of a life yet here I stand.

I knew my plight, saw the light,
now I strive 2 no longer do what's wrong but what's right.

So many people I ran with got caught up in the game -- wanting all the bling bling
and a so-called name
not realizing we're all just pawns in
1 big chess game.

I recall telling certain cats the number I wanted off of every package.
Truth B told I was blind, deaf, and dumb moven a$$ backwards livin' life as a savage.

I was that cat u read about, and
that so many thugs claim 2b about.

Had a lil girl then started 2 realize I need 2 get up out
the game n do right.
My crew took a fall yet I stand tall:
1 is doing time who always thought he was super bad--
now he's in the feds trying 2 keep cats from getting up in that a$$.

One lost his wife, another turned snitch.
Another couldn't leave drugs alone and went from pushen coke 2 using that sh!t.

Oh as 4 me, I've been out the game,
and I'm never going back to that life.
I just live right.
And feel Blessed 2 have my children and a wonderful wife.

Blessed

Within your eyes I have come 2c that we are truly meant 2b.
From your lips u have touched the depths of this man's very being like no other.

Within your smile lies that remedy that makes my gray skies blue.
U are my equal, my other half never shall
u B treated like a whore.

Within life not many are as blessed 2 have a woman such as u, I'd B more then a fool,
if I were 2 ever loose u.

A good woman, a perfect woman
is so hard 2 find.
I'm not 1 2 place any limitations on u,
4 I am a witness that u do have a mind.

From your unlimited knowledge and wisdom u have given methe earthly understanding
that at times are needed ,
so that I may not let life's trials and tribulations get me down.

4 in sickness and in health baby,
4 richer and 4 poorer u have been there 4 me.
U are a strong Blackwoman with a big heart.

We have been 2gether 4 years had our share of good times and dried each other tears;
I am blessed 2 have u in my life as my best friend, supreme lover, woman, queen
and my Beloved wife.

The Love of A Blackman
(A sermon of the heart)

I would like 2 now define the love of a Blackman.
The love of such a Blackman is 1 that cannot B measured by time and space.
It is a love that u may not only feel from the depths of your very being,
but see as well as taste.

The love of a Blackman is when he has come 2 realize just how blessed he is
2 have a strong, intelligent Blackwoman in his life, he let's her know in any and every way
that he loves her.
Never neglecting her but respecting her,
never limiting her, but supporting her.

The love of a Blackman is
when he has come 2 know
that u are all that he needs
and could ever want;
2 the point where he could not eat nor sleep
4 you're on his mind
and without u life would not b worth living.

The love of a Blackman is 1 of great trust leaving no room 2 ever doubt each other.
The love of a Blackman is when he is willing
2 accept his Black woman
4 who and what she is;
never attempting 2 make her n2
some1 she is not.
2 lift her up when others may put her down.
2b there even if it's just 2 listen.

The love of a Blackman is when he knows that this beautiful Black woman
is his true soul mate, and in time she will B his wife; as well as bear their children.

The love of a Blackman 4 his woman
is 1 that has no limitations.
Though they may have their differences
like all couples do--
He knows that it's best 2 always talk it out
rather then fight it out.
(cont.)

Within life there is somebody 4 everybody, though no1 is perfect, he or she may just B the 1 that gives u the love u rightfully deserve.
This is The Love of a Blackman.

True Woman

Yes Blackwoman u are the perfect woman 4 me, u are one of god's best creations.
U know what I want, as well as my every need, at times putting yours aside so that I may be happy.

U are a true woman, 1 having knowledge, wisdom, understanding, culture and refinement.
Time and time again u have shown and proven that u are mine, 2 have and hold in sickness and health 4 richer and poorer.

If 1 of us is 2 return 2 the essence,
then we shall remain 2gether
in the mental or spiritual form.

U are a true woman, 4 it is your understanding that has shown me that your criticism of my ways and actions,
will only help 2 make me a better Blackman.

I looked past the beautiful face, pretty smile and your wonderful physical form and came 2c u 4 who as well as what u truly are.

I think of u daily, and recognize u 4 the strong Blackwoman that u are.
U are a woman of great intelligence, putting an end 2 the myth that u are limited.

This may be a man's world in the eyes of many, but it would B nothing
if not 4 the Blackwoman.

Within life, I've faced many trials and tribulations; and just when I thought I was down 4 the count,
u were there giving me the strength 2 get up.

The weight u uphold is heavy.
There are times when it seems you are not able, yet u keep everything around u in motion, work, school,
our beautiful children and your husband.
As I think back 4 a moment, just a few years ago, I was so stressed over
what I thought was love.

(cont.)

U are a true woman, despite those snakes and blood suckers who have called themselves
men within your presence, only seeing u 4 what u lower half had 2 offer them, who never
acknowledged that within your divine body also dwelled a mind.
Blackwoman, from the depths of my being,
do I love u.
I will B there 4 u now and 4ever after.

We may have our differences and may not agree on everything, but there is 1 thing we will
always agree on and that is
our love 4 each other.

My Precious Jewel

"Fertile" within u many seeds have been planted;
and over the course of time they have,
and will become the true kings/queens that they righteously are.

All of the above holds much weight on the original man and all has been made understood.
I dealt with the mental b4 I entered n2 the darkness of your womb.
U have comforted me like no other, at times being the mother that I needed
never once looking 4 love else where.
When all that u could ever need nor want is right at home.

Through the blood, sweat and tears I suffered in attempts 2b the man I once was.
What I have experienced is nothing
compared 2 what u have gone through over the years Nefertari.

U came 2 me looking past the marks where shackles once were.
Even in this day and time beautiful,
u are disrespected as well as mistreated,

not only by those who used u as a tool but even by those who advocated 2 love u.

U have been the center of my very being but due 2 my being on a paper chase,
I started slipping.
I shall b there 4 u always love as u 4 me
4 u are indeed my precious jewel.

Thank U Baby

My love, there could B no other love like the love u have given me.
U were there when my children's mother choose 2b with another woman
and damn near crushed my heart.
U came n2 my life at a time when I had somewhat slipped but not yet fallen
due 2 a female who just wasn't good 4 me.
U came n2 my life at a time when I didn't have much but open arms, yet your love made
me feel as if I was on top of the world;
U were there 4 me as I went from
this girl 2 that girl.

Here it is years later, and people just can't stop looking at your finger,
4 our cipher is complete and we're doing our thing; wasn't letting you go so I made that
move, saying good by New York and hello 2 Complete Happiness 4 I wanted 2b with u.

I love u and this comes from the depths of this Blackman's heart. I fast and build that we
shall never part. I know others have given u reason 2 question a Blackman's
love in the past,
yet rest assured that this man does love u more than words could ever define;
with all my heart, soul, body and mind.

I Pray

I pray 4 our love 2b more than enough 2 get us through the roughest of storms.
I pray that u are strong during the times that I am gone providing food, clothing and shelter
4 our happy lil home.

I pray that u realize that I'm blessed 2 have u in my life as my best friend, woman and wife.
I pray that I'm there whenever u need me, be it anytime of the day or night.
I pray that we're 2 busy making love
2 make time 2 fight.

I pray that the love and trust we have never fades, and that u and I will B 2gether
way beyond our dying day.

I pray that I never B the reason 2 bring tears.
I pray that the sun shines on all that u do.
I pray that u know I love u and that u know that 2 me u will always B beautiful.
I pray u know, if I never told u b4, I need u.

So after all the trouble, drama, pain and crazy women in my life it took sometime B4 I came 2 realize there was nothing keeping me in NYC, So I packed my bags not caring if others thought it was wrong or if it was right.
I needed 2b with the 1 person who had always brought happiness 2 my life, 2 make a long story short I crossed that line and now she's my wife ☺

Beloved Sha

No more Tears

Yes, no more tears no more fears and I owe it all 2 the woman who stood by a brotha 4 so many years.
So now I have no more drama
and no more fights,
or lonely nights.
A brotha is where he wants 2b
and needs 2b.
I have a real woman, a good woman, who loves me 4 me.
And after realizing that, we both let go of the past and got married.

Life with my wife is in no way the same as it was with any of those females b4 her.
A brotha has to keep it real and just say I adore her

I would have 2 say it's so much better,
4 when sh!t got rough and things seemed tough, it was this strong Blackwoman
who showed she cared,
And showed she was there 4 me.

So no more tears, no more lies, I'm blessed and she's the reason why.
My wife's love is the reason I smile and no longer cry.

Sweet Dreams

As I step out of all that I'm wearing n2 your darkness
I close my Eyes and become wet within your love.

Beloved Sha

About the Author

Beloved Sha is a writer, husband, and father born and raised in the fast and often brutal streets of Brooklyn, NY who has made his home in Columbus, Ohio. Chocolate Tears/Tears No More is his second published work, and his first published book. For more from Beloved Sha, you can write to him at: belovedsha@firstbornpublishing.com visit his page at
Http://www.firstbornpublishing.com/belovedsha

www.ingramcontent.com/pod-product-compliance
Ingram Content Group UK Ltd.
Pitfield, Milton Keynes, MK11 3LW, UK
UKHW051303180426
11947UKWH00020B/1880